IT'S TIME TO LEGALIZE ALL DRUGS

WALTER RANDALL BANNISTER

TABLE OF CONTENTS

1
REPEAL ALL DRUG LAWS CREATING "CRIMES" WITHOUT VICTIMS

I support the protections provided by the Fourth Amendment to be secure in our persons, homes, and property. Only actions that infringe on the rights of others can properly be termed crimes. I favor the repeal of all laws creating "crimes" without victims, such as the use of drugs for medicinal or recreational purposes.

2
THE WAR ON DRUGS THREATENS INDIVIDUAL LIBERTIES

The War on Drugs is a threat to individual liberty and domestic order; furthermore, it has provided a rationale by which the power of the state has been expanded to restrict our privacy. I condemn the use of "profiles" as sufficient to satisfy the probable cause requirement of the Fourth Amendment, the use of "civil asset forfeiture" to reduce the standard of proof historically borne by government in prosecutions, and the use of military forces for civilian law enforcement.

3
IT IS TIME TO LEGALIZE ALL DRUGS

People have a right to ingest/smoke whatever they want and to explore the contents of "their own mind" in the PROCESS, so long as they are not hurting anyone else, even if it kills them. This is a human right, albeit one that few people think of.

Imagine if you had the right to have a shed in YOUR backyard but you didn't have a right to explore the contents of that shed. That would be a little insulting, wouldn't it?

Those who want to limit our mental exploration are to be held highly suspect. Those same people, for instance, often advocate that perfectly normal and healthy individuals go on 7 psychotropic pharmaceuticals at the same time. Limiting access to information is usually a form of domination.

We don't truly have access to our own minds right now. Some of us do, but there is a huge effort to dumb all of us down and re-engineering us. Fluoride in our water supply destroying our third eye (pineal gland) is just one of many examples of this.

Decriminalization of pot is a sad effort to appease control freaks. I see no reason to demand anything SHORT of full-on legalization (of all drugs).

The nanny-state should get off of our backs. Waving its finger, the state pretends it's looking out for our best interest but half the time it's dealing the very drugs that it's punishing people for possessing.

Drugs are prohibited in ORDER to instill a monopoly (e.g. coke/heroin) and/or to mold a society's consciousness (e.g. magic mushrooms, LSD, DMT).

State-owned EDUCATION and the mainstream media are the mouthpieces of the government and that is bad enough but we should now (or sometime soon) also deal with the reality that social engineers have prohibited specific substances precisely because those substances have, for thousands of years (in many cases), helped people become more self-aware, helped people discover that the ego is an illusion and that the true self knows no borders.

Drugs are prohibited in ORDER to instill a monopoly (e.g. coke/heroin) and/or to mold a society's consciousness (e.g. magic mushrooms, LSD, DMT).

State-owned EDUCATION and the mainstream media are the mouthpieces of the government and that is bad enough but we should now (or sometime soon) also deal with the reality that social engineers have prohibited specific substances precisely because those substances have, for thousands of years (in many cases), helped people become more self-aware, helped people discover that the ego is an illusion and that the true self knows no borders.

Whether this discovery happens rapidly via a deep introspective journey fomented by a heroic dose of magic mushrooms or whether a slower but slightly similar PROCESS unfolds over time with the aid of the occasional toke of a flower that allows one to relax and decompress, the name of the game is self-discovery and elites seem to passionately hate this game.

While this is technically an insane and sinister state of affairs – and, of course, those guilty should be held ACCOUNTABLE – I personally think we need to clean up our act a little bit and look in the mirror, especially with respect to how we treat each other and how we dominate the other creatures that inhabit this planet. Otherwise we will have simply learned nothing, can easily be shown to be inconsistent and at that point we cannot expect to be taken seriously.

4
MISGUIDED RAGE

If you are one of those people who puts their blind trust in a government, you might find yourself at a soccer riot, filled with rage, fighting with someone over a ball going into a net, ignoring the true culprits behind the shaping of YOUR depressing life, all just because you listened when they (government/society) told you "we know what's best for you" and because you had not yet made the decision to face the reality that you had no sound reason to believe them (I'm not saying it's an easy decision, I'm just saying it's a decision... one that you likely can still make).

The pharmaceutical industry MAKES MORE MONEY when people are ignorant of the fact that marijuana & hemp can replace a lot of the "traditional" drugs out there (and indeed, hemp does represent a massive threat to the oil industry as well) but at the end of the day elites are really giving each other high fives over the fact that they've more-or-less successfully banned one of the most awesome things in the world.

Pot is illegal because pot is absolutely amazing and has the ability to dramatically improve many different aspects of YOUR life in a variety of different ways.

It's great that people are fighting so hard for patients to be able to get effective medicine, but where does that put those of us who just want to have a good time with that same medicine? And wouldn't those who want their medicine also benefit from the efforts of those who want total freedom to enjoy that which is harmless?

Do I have to sit here and wish I get cancer or some other serious ailment just so I can one day finally enjoy smoking a joint in peace? This is absurd.

Comedian Doug Stanhope eloquently echoes my initial point, that the real problem is one of individual rights: "If you're gonna have a pro-drug argument, start the argument where it starts: I have the right to do what ever the hell I want to my own body, if it kills me slowly, happy for me, f*ck you, "clack clack" (miming a pump-action shotgun) stop me!"

When I came across the headline, "Snoop Dogg's marijuana drug bust highlights idiocy of the failed War on Drugs," I was happy that Natural News was reporting on such a blatant attack on individual rights. I mean Snoop did have a medical marijuana license, when all is said and done, and these mixed messages about pot are getting ridiculous. When I finally had time to actually read the article a week later, however, I was shocked and amazed.

A Drug Court For Pot?
The article states,
Ideally, marijuana possession should be de-criminalized to FREE up law enforcement resources for more important tasks (and to take the ego out of the DEA, which is a rogue government agency gang that OPENLY violates state law). Barring that, the next best option is to pass state laws that put marijuana possession under the jurisdiction of a drug court, not a criminal court. In fact, this idea of approaching drug possession from a HEALTH CARE point of view (rather than a criminal point of view) works for all street drugs: meth, heroin, cocaine, etc.

Later the article elaborates on the drug court:

Drug problems needed to be treated in a "drug court" where court options include:

- Mandatory drug detox treatment.

- Mandatory drug counseling.

- Nutritional support programs for detox and overcoming drug addiction.

- Paying of relatively small fines, similar to traffic tickets.

- Regular drug testing for a limited period of time to determine compliance.

My first thought is, "are you joking?"

court, not a criminal court. In fact, this idea of approaching drug possession from a HEALTH CARE point of view (rather than a criminal point of view) works for all street drugs: meth, heroin, cocaine, etc.

Later the article elaborates on the drug court:
Drug problems needed to be treated in a "drug court" where court options include:

- Mandatory drug detox treatment.
Mandatory drug counseling.
- Nutritional support programs for detox and overcoming drug addiction.
- Paying of relatively small fines, similar to traffic tickets.
- Regular drug testing for a limited period of time to determine compliance.

My first thought is, "are you joking?"

My second thought is, "why not make all drugs legal?"

This probably only sounds radical to those who have a

residue of a holier-than-thou attitude whereby they think they know what's best for everyone. To me, a drug court for pot sounds radical.

Freedom is an all-or-nothing thing. You can't be a half-slave.

As many people have pointed out, decriminalization is a flimsy concept. I almost find the concept offensive. It's saying you can have "small amounts". What a tease! There is no dignity in decriminalization and it only delays the inevitable.

There is no dignity in decriminalization and it only delays the inevitable.

Also, I don't know if Mike Adams forgot, but it's worth mentioning that marijuana is not only "far less harmful" than alcohol, as he put it, but marijuana is also a medicine that treats over 100 conditions. I don't say that as an argument for legalization. This is simply something which Natural News has covered before but which is apparently irrelevant now (although, to be fair, he didn't write the specific Natural News article I'm thinking of).

Personally, I think it would have been ideal if Mike Adams mentioned operation Fast and Furious (which he has covered before), as globalist-funded coke gangs spilling into the US with guns given to them by the ATF and the White House would definitely be relevant to a discussion of the root causes of drug-culture.

The current marijuana situation is a joke. The whole drug war is a joke. They ship the narcotics in and then bust us for using them. There's no bargaining with these people. If you give them an inch, they'll take a mile.

This whole thing is a very complex issue and deserves a lot of attention. We are at a particular stage in our evolution. Our relationship to each other and our relationship to the world is reflected accordingly. We cannot reasonably hope to reclaim our humanity while simultaneously allowing others to use every excuse they can come up with to dictate the parameters of our behavior and mental exploration. We do not need to be treated like infants.

Let's pause for a moment to examine one thing. When you spend your time with friends and family, you start to sound like them. We all know that.

Similarly, we are trapped, so to speak, in a Matrix-like world that is constructed by unseen cockroaches, and so those cockroaches have rubbed off on us.

I mean, it seems like the powers-that-be think they know what's best for everyone and everything. It follows that we'll mimic their dominating ways when exposed to the constructed reality they have manufactured for us (at least a bit, in some ways, I mean they're not our "friends" but you catch my drift).

It's not all bad. Conversely, the evil scumbags must also have the good people rub off on them. It's only a matter of time before the nanny-state gains a bit of sanity and we all understand where we're all coming from.

While doing more research, I found an earlier Natural News article about Willie Nelson's arrest for pot, where Mike Adams advocated legalization (and taxation... I don't understand why we should tax this... maybe I'm missing something but I'm going to ignore this for now).

Legalization seems to be a much more sound position but

I don't know why a little more than a year later Mike Adams became content demanding the above mentioned de-criminalization / drug court (which I feel represents a compromise).

In this article on the Willie Nelson bust, Mike writes, For the record, I'm not a marijuana smoker, and I would never encourage any individual to take up such a habit unless they had a legitimate medical need for pain relief.

However, I am totally against the continued persecution of individuals who buy, possess or consume this medicinal herb. They harm no one but themselves, and smoking marijuana produces side effects that are far milder than drinking alcohol.

I find the "harm no one but themselves" part to be a little pompous. Personally, I would recommend that everyone try it at least once. There, I said it. I'm also not the only person who's said it.

Legendary comedian Bill Hicks has joked that marijuana should not only be legalized but should also be mandatory Comedian Kat Williams also gets the message across very succinctly:

It helps me make visual art and music, it helps me write articles, and above all, it helps me be more patient and understanding with people. Perhaps as a result of a combination of all of these things, it helps me be more self-aware and allows me to not waste my energy fighting other peoples' battles.

Influential writer Alan Watts was largely responsible for

popularizing Zen in the west and he has said that a lot of the problems in life occur simply from not thinking things through all the way to the end.

Marijuana helps many people slow down and not panic so much, to the point that we can actually think for once. State-owned education seeks to accomplish the opposite of this and that's an important thing to keep in mind. Your government wants you in the dark about substances that make you less afraid.

Mike Adams goes on to write things which are indeed 100% accurate but which nevertheless don't capture the whole picture:

Why is marijuana criminalized in America? The answer is simply that marijuana prohibition is the cornerstone of the American police state. Keeping this herb illegal keeps millions of people employed in law enforcement who otherwise wouldn't have jobs. It keeps the prison industry strong and gives cops a reason to search vehicles.

It even gives law enforcement officers yet another excuse to hold "terrorism drills." Seriously: A recent terrorism drill in Northern California imagined pot heads taking over Shasta Dam and blowing up vehicles These cops must have a lot of free time on their hands to dream up these wild (and highly improbable) scenarios. But keeping marijuana criminalized allows them to spend more taxpayer money running these useless drills that, after all, keep them all well paid.

At the same time, it causes billions of dollars a year to flow into the underground black market economy — money that would otherwise be used to raise tax revenues for states.

Yes, these are all true reasons. In fact, even in Arnprior, Ontario, Canada, back in April of 2011, police threw a flash-bang grenade into a guy's son's bedroom window (for suspicion of some pot and a weapon) and the guy even turned out to be the wrong guy. The cops were at the wrong house. If that man's son was asleep in that bed he could have been killed.

I agree that police do need an excuse to push people around these days but they're not just picking some random excuse. It's not just a happy coincidence that this particular excuse has to do with a drug which, as I mentioned before, helps people make art and write (books, plays, films, documentaries, reports, articles, etc.), helps them think/meditate, and helps to dissolve the ego. Did I mention it helps people love each other? Is that a medicinal benefit?

5
A MOUNTAIN OF LAWS

It's worth noting that I was surprised to even find out that there was a time when people could drive cars without a "driver's license" (and then I was surprised at the fact that I was surprised). Many years ago when I visited France I was shocked to see that their laws are such that they allowed 16 year old kids to purchase alcohol at the corner store. They allowed you to drink in a car as long as you were a passenger and not the driver. They also allowed people to drink outside on the streets. In Canada, the laws were a lot less lenient and yet I saw more car accidents, more teenagers getting drunk for the sake of getting drunk, more drinkers making fools of themselves on the streets, etc.

We must get rid of this idea that we have some sort of right to put a law on everything, every human activity. Simply saying, "It's for the greater good", is not sufficient. Those who purport this overreach often say they're doing so for our best interest but any sensible person has witnessed the pattern that has emanated from the tentacles of the machine/cabal driving this accelerating global tyranny and it is an ugly pattern.

In fact, when one reads the writings of influential elites like Edward Bernays, one gets the overwhelming impression that he's trying to convince everyone that if they didn't allow society to be run by "men we've never heard of" tragedy would follow. Compartmentalization is the kind of thing that allows a disgusting Brave New World like ours to run smoothly.

Of course, by running smoothly I mean that we remain seemingly eternally ignorant of our true nature and of what/who we really are, our astronomical potential for true progress, and we get closer and closer to assimilating the traits of those who dominate us, we continue to allow our energy to be drained and our lifeblood to be sucked out of us, until we no longer recognize ourselves. That's what "running smoothly" really is to people like Edward Bernays.

I'd like to think that now, in 2015, we're past this naive attitude and can see the organic nature of our existence. Not everybody is a good drinker but laws aren't the solution to that. I don't know if there is a "top-down" solution to that kind of problem. I have a strong hunch that things like that come down to personal responsibility. You can't make a law, for example, saying "everybody is allowed to drink... except Jeff... Jeff sucks at drinking so he's not allowed".

Imagine if that's what the law actually said. That would be insane.

Why? Because Jeff is not the only bad drinker and you can't keep track of all the bad drinkers. Even if you could keep track of them, wouldn't you have better things to do with your time? It doesn't matter if Jeff's a bad drinker. It doesn't matter if everybody's a bad drinker. The law isn't there to make everybody perfect in every way.

Adding laws shouldn't be a pastime. It shouldn't be something you do for fun. In fact, history tells us that it's best to have as few laws as possible.

You are not their God. You don't own them. The only reasonable thing to do is to let everybody drink despite the fact that a few people might ruin that freedom for the rest. And historically, that's what has happened. If a person can't control himself, no nanny-state is going to teach him to control himself by controlling him for him. I'm not saying, "abolish the drinking and driving laws" or anything like that, but can anybody remember how well the prohibition of alcohol worked? How well do you think people would have taken to alcohol being regulated by a special drug court?

the prohibition of alcohol worked? How well do you think people would have taken to alcohol being regulated by a special drug court?

A baby is not going to learn how to walk if you don't give him/her a chance to walk.

With all this in mind, however, even though we have not shed this naive attitude, I will remind all of you that it is not a hindrance that few people think of this, for indeed times of great change are often ushered in by an irate minority. Remember that.

6
COCAINE = SPEED = RITALIN = COFFEE

Another thought I had after reading the suggestion to have a drug court regulating pot is that I can't count how many people I've seen lose a big chunk of their humanity simply from ingesting coffee all the time.

An argument that is sometimes given for the prohibition of these "harder" drugs is that people end up stealing to support their habit. First of all, caffeine is a drug. If coffee or cigarettes were very expensive, perhaps we'd see many more segments of the population stealing to support those habits as well (and indeed as the economy turns to crap, people will start to steal food from each other... is that any reason to outlaw food?)

The real reason that truly destructive narcotics like cocaine are illegal in the first place has nothing to do with the fact that cocaine may lead to destructive behaviour and nothing to do with any possible altruism on the part of your government. The reason harder (and more useless) drugs like cocaine are illegal is, again, to impose a monopoly on the narcotics.

Drug dealers generally don't like that they might go to jail, but I'd be willing to bet that at least some of them love the cash they get to keep when they successfully stay out of jail and they might also love the price inflation that occurs when one of their "peers" (who they didn't know, maybe) gets locked up.

Mike Adams was indeed accurate in raising the point that there is little difference between drugs like Ritalin vs. cocaine or meth (or what was likely cocaine that dealers diluted with "incense powder", baking soda, or other cocaine-looking things — another reason to legalize all drugs). A Ritalin high feels almost identical to the cocaine high. That's right, folks. Most of these ignorant parents are basically giving their 9 year old kids cocaine in the form of Ritalin.

This happening all while the parents are completely oblivious that the coffee they drink every day produces the same effects/feelings as cocaine as well. People treat coffee like it's water.

I've heard of people trying to "sober up", after a night of drinking, by ingesting caffeine (as though being high on coffee is sobriety). Similarly, I've seen cocaine work wonders with respect to "sobering" drunk people up. A guy who is so drunk that he can barely walk or talk is literally a line or two away from coming off as though he has had almost no alcohol the entire night. I've seen this happen.

While things like speed are more synthetic, the feeling of the high is basically the same. It is a travesty that so few people are aware of these things. Maybe someone more versed in chemistry would be able to split hairs here, but alas, the feeling of the high for these drugs is dauntingly similar.

Remember cocaine was once an ingredient in Coca Cola?

7
PERSONAL RESPONSIBILITY

I'm not going to lie – the pharmaceutical drug ads on TV are not helping the situation but I don't think we have a drug culture because of ads on television. I submit to you that we have a drug culture because we want to have a drug culture.

Maybe we have a drug culture because drugs distract people and everyone's too lazy and lacking in foresight to actually deal with the world's problems. Maybe we choose to sedate ourselves and our children because we fear the responsibility we would have to take on when we realize how powerful we really are. We have this vague feeling that the longer we've thought a certain way the harder it is to change, however, I think too many people barely ever even try to change.

It seems to me that making it illegal to put drug advertisements on television would be a giant waste of time. Nobody (except for maybe victims of MK Ultra or some cruel thing like that) is forced at gunpoint to watch television. In general, we sit and waste our lives via our own free will. Let's own up to that. We almost love the propaganda. More laws is not the answer.

Raising your child is your responsibility, not the TV's responsibility and not the state's responsibility. In fact, this type of Orwellian thought is the very reason the dictator in the novel 1984 is named "Big Brother". It gets you used to the idea of feeling like you can trust the state and that it can replace your family. Arguably, globalists have been fairly successful in destroying the family and indeed this is one of their multifaceted tactics of global domination.

8
LET'S GET REAL

Let's stop pretending we're that different from the people who dominate us. We should set an example and be the change we want to see.

Why are we so surprised?

Many of us now believe in karma, after all. How many of you have a cat that you've mutilated, euphemistically referring to that act as "spaying" or "fixing"? Hey, I'm not saying I'm better than you. I once got a veterinarian to "fix" a cat that I had too (when I was living on "auto-pilot" more). I'm just saying let's be honest with ourselves. How many of you have allowed your son (or daughter, in some places) to be victims of the barbaric act of circumcision?

How many of you have a gold fish in a tiny glass jail in your house?

How many of you don't give two sh!ts when you see those poor lobsters at the grocery store living in conditions that I would call torture, as they are forced to be surrounded by their own crap and urine in a fluoride filled tank with their claws clamped shut, all these lobsters on top of one another in a mountain of misery, staring at artificial lights as they count down the days they have left?

You might think that's funny or irrelevant, but in a world that is pure consciousness your intentions or negligence have an instantaneous affect on everything. You're putting out bad vibes by not looking at the facts.

Sure, many other animals suffer as a result of stores like

these existing and it's definitely not always in-your-face like with the lobsters – people have the opportunity to separate "beef" from "cow" in this way – but I have never met anyone who has even mentioned this lobster abuse to me or what they think of it. I've seen people in front of fancy restaurants protesting with signs against foie gras being served (as they should – foie gras is an abomination), but never any love for the lobsters.
The fact that we can put up with this level of abuse right in front of our faces is, I think, a huge part of the problem. Just walking into a pet-store should kill anyone's mood, but for some reason it doesn't.

When I was young, I had a neighbour who "owned" a dog. The neighbour would let the small dog roam around in a tiny fenced-in jail-like area in the backyard but the dog also had some sort of electronic device on its collar that seemed to automatically electrocute the poor thing every time it barked. I would often hear the dog try to bark and then I would instantly hear the loud high pitched cry of pain that it let out upon getting zapped/tazed.

I have more stories like this, but I think you get the picture. When I came across the headline "Marijuana Prevents PTSD In Rats" I thought two things:

#1: How the hell would anybody give post-traumatic stress disorder to a rat?

#2: Do you really need to torture rats to find out pot's effectiveness? I mean, it doesn't grow everywhere for nothing and I'm sure you could have found many humans who had PTSD and simply asked them, "Does pot help you?"

Equally important to scrutinizing the power structure of

our civilization is our ability respect each other in the moment, on a day to day basis, so that we can remember what it is we're trying to save in the first place.

It is in our best interest to act humanely to all the different creatures and spirits that inhabit our planet. Otherwise we are chasing our tails and we can look forward to wasting even more energy on a fabricated war on drugs that only serves to divide and conquer us.

www.ingramcontent.com/pod-product-compliance
Lightning Source LLC
Chambersburg PA
CBHW070258300526
45791CB00022B/1642